Songs of Ourselves
Volume 2

A STUDY GUIDE
on 14 Set Poems for 2016-2018

(14 Model Responses with 77 IGCSE Exam Style Questions)

William Blake, 'Clod and Pebble'
Lady Mary Wroth, 'Song'
Kathleen Raine, 'Passion'
George Herbert, 'Love'
John Donne, 'Love's Infiniteness'
William Wordsworth, 'She was a Phantom of Delight'
Emma Jones, 'Tiger in the Menagerie'
Amanda Chong, 'Lion Heart'
Edith Sitwell, 'Heart and Mind'
Liz Lochhead, 'For my Grandmother Knitting'
Dilip Chitre, 'Father Returning Home'
Patricia Beer, 'The Lost Woman'
Owen Sheers, 'Coming Home'
Sam Hunt, 'Stabat Mater'

Atchula Subrahmanyam

ISBN: 1522922784
ISBN-13: 978-1522922780

DEDICATION

I dedicate this book to all my students who taught me how to teach.

CONTENTS

	Acknowledgments	i
1	The Clod and the Pebble by William Blake	3-6
2	Song by Lady Mary Wroth	7-10
3	Passion by Kathleen Raine	11-15
4	Love by George Herbert	16-20
5	Love's Infiniteness by John Donne	21-25
6	She was a Phantom of Delight by William Wordsworth	26-30
7	Tiger in the Menagerie by Emma Jones	31-35
8	Lion Heart by Amanda Chong	36-40
9	Heart and Mind by Edith Sitwell	41-45
10	For my Grandmother Knitting by Liz Lochhead	46-50
11	Father Returning Home by Dilip Chitre	51-56
12	The Lost Woman by Patricia Beer	57-61
13	Coming Home by Owen Sheers	62-66
14	Stabat Mater by Sam Hunt	67-71

ACKNOWLEDGMENTS

I would like to thank all my teachers who taught me and shaped my life.

1 THE CLOD AND THE PEBBLE by William Blake

IGCSE Exam Style Questions:

1. Explore how Blake vividly portrays contradictory views of love in the poem *The Clod and the Pebble*.

    OR

2. How does Blake vividly portray the two different perspectives of love in the poem *The Clod and the Pebble?*

    OR

3. Explore how Blake vividly portrays the experience and innocence of love in the poem *The Clod and the Pebble*.

Model Response: A Grade

Explore how Blake vividly portrays the experience and innocence of love in poem The Clod and the Pebble.

Blake's poem 'The cold and the Pebble' vividly explores the poet's philosophy of love and how love is perceived by human experiences. Blake's portrayal of love is enchanting in the way he treats the clod and the pebble as human beings with emotions of love. The treatment of human spirit given to these characters makes the poem vivid and enables to convey the perspectives of love for the reader.

The poet profoundly presents the idea of love both as selfless and selfish virtues. However, the subject of love rises as a pure and genuine emotion of life in the readers mind. The clod succinctly brings faith in 'love' as a wave of emotion which comforts others around. The song 'sung' by 'little clod' leaves bigger impact on the readers to believe that it gives but never expects anything for 'itself'. Thus, the clod becomes a symbol of innocence and 'love' which inspires the readers to note the true meaning of love in life. The poet's abstract treatment selflessness and selfishness couples with characters that describe the idea of love so vivid.

In the first stanza, it is interesting to note that Blake significantly portrays divine relation between love and heaven. It is axiomatic description of the poet to state that the presence of 'love' creates the atmosphere of 'Heaven'. The clod makes it possible to build the spiritual and pure place of heaven as it doesn't please itself to 'build' heaven because it sacrifices all its 'care' and comfort to provide ease to build heaven. The introduction of 'Hell' and 'Heaven' in the poem indicates the fact that the religious allusion is brought to present the beliefs of the poet. Therefore, the poet exuberantly proposes the idea that giving is heaven but not taking.

In the second stanza, Blake surprises the readers describing and relating certain attributes of love to human actions. Even though the innocent 'clod' never experiences 'ease' and 'delight', it preaches and sings the song of being altruistic and suffers enormous pain. Despite the clod is being crushed 'under the cattle's feet', it remains forgiving and flexible and holds a very positive outlook of 'love' in life. The poet personifies the clod into a human character that is 'trodden' with heavy force yet it displays positive attributes of love and human life. Hence, the poet significantly claims that the idea of love as matter of character in the being.

Considering the setting in the poem, it is quite intriguing to note how both clod and pebble give a greater insight to the reader. The living conditions of the clod and pebble differ so their outlook in life seems different. Despite being 'trodden' by the 'cattle's feet', the clod exuberantly sings its joy of 'love'; which is extremely divine in its nature. On the other hand, it is appalling to note how clod defines love so high even after its agonising setting and immense pain. The poet shifts and brings abruptness with the conjunction 'but' to suggest how maturity of pebble shatters innocent definition by clod of love. The setting of 'brook' for the pebble is so soothing and relaxing however it draws its meaning of love as its 'meters meet' (definition of love created) but differs from clod' kind definition. Thus, Blake shapes the meaning of love through the setting in the poem.

Further into the poem, readers closely identify the contrary perceptions of love in both clod and pebble. The poet's wisdom enlightens the readers to understand the different ways of holdings the convictions of love. However, it is primarily evident to note that both 'clod and pebble' find 'delight' and joy despite their attitude towards 'love'. But the attitude of pebble shapes out of experience results in 'loss of ease' to others where as the clod sacrifices its 'ease to another'. Thus, the joy echoes more from the tone of clod than the pebble so it all depends on how one attempts to achieve them. The means of this achievement changes the value of love in life.

Next, the poet conveys not only the idea of love but finds a correlation between masculine and feminine love. Readers note the poet's idea of portraying how the genders also hold a variation in their perception of love. The hard and unchanged 'pebble' with experience represents masculine love that joys and causes 'loss' to 'build hell' despite 'heaven's presence. On the other hand, the optimistic 'clod' of 'clay' symbolises itself as feminine in nature with purity in mind but bears pain and sacrifices everything for 'another'. Therefore, the poet attempts to state that perception of love not only changes with the character of a person but also the gender of the person.

In conclusion the poet shares his deep wisdom and ideas of love; which are held high in innocent and altruistic heart as clod, but the pebble seems to exploit its experience for its own delight. The poet makes a point in the end that the convictions, virtues and gender differences do change the perception of love in the man.   **Word Count: 843**

2 *SONG* by Lady Mary Wroth

IGCSE Exam Style Questions:

1. Explore how Wroth intriguingly portrays the virtues of love in the poem *Song.*

   OR

2. Explore how Wroth intriguingly portrays the nature of love in the poem *Song.*

   OR

3. In what ways Wroth compares child's behaviour to the emotion of love in the poem *Song* .

   OR

4. How does Wroth intriguingly personifies the love in the poem *Song*?

OR

5. In what ways Wroth intriguingly conveys the negativity of love in the poem *Song*.

Model Response: A Grade

Explore how Wroth intriguingly portrays the virtues of love in the poem Song.

In the poem Song, Wroth critically portrays the inglorious character of the personified love and establishes a negative cliché portraying the pain and inevitable submission to the sentiment of soft emotion when making love and being in love . Wroth's Song elaborates on the adversaries experienced by *the being* in love who is supposedly implied to be female awaiting reasonable reciprocation from him or an emotion of love itself. Wroth's portrayal lists a numerous defective virtues of love (he) whose sole aim is to seek self-pleasure and cause mere pain.

In the second stanza of the poem, Wroth vividly throws light on the virtue of love's fidelity and reliability when it comes to 'trust' and promise in the emotion of love. In bringing out this character of desirous nature of love, the poet's hyperbolic description cuts its image of 'no measure' for desire therefore it is his virtue of 'folly'. The poet explicitly draws a sketch of love's character which cannot be trusted of 'not one word that he speaketh' or what he 'promiseth'. Wroth evidently conveys that there is no possibility of keeping the promise and a sign of loyalty from the being in love and without doubt the promise will be broken in the end to inflict pain.

Wroth severely cautions the true nature of the double-faced love that is powered with affection, sentiment as well as virtue of sweet pain that he can inflict *the being or emotion* (a person's inner self). The poet's idea is to separate the love as an emotion and a female to show how both are affected by the personified 'child' or 'him'. The emotion of love always stands extremely wanting like a glutton for 'more craving' and pleasure that love seeks in its relation thereupon he is 'never satisfied with having'. The love is shown as an emotion that does not deserve any great praise depicting the absurdity and 'endless folly'. So the exaggeration of its cravings is in its true virtue of betrayal and abandonment when pleased. In brief, the poet closes the idea that love is truly disguised emotion that is never realised being in love and needs to be chased and given more; expecting nothing and experiencing emotional emptiness.

In the third stanza of the poem, Wroth intriguingly depicts deception and betrayal as the characteristics of love and its emotion. The poet interests the readers in the ideas of how *the being* experiences the love and goes through the emotion of sweetness of love only to 'cozen' and 'flatter'. Wroth delineates the sweetness of love and its soft sentiment 'vow nothing but false matter' leading to deception and betrayal. The use of second person plural pronoun 'you' evidently addresses the readers and conveys a clear message of love's deceptive nature. The readers seem to be baffled by the idea of leaving and gaining the 'glory' to be his. Therefore, the poet stresses on a tragic element of emotion of love that is implied and never realised when in love.

Towards the end of the fourth stanza, Wroth paints the emotion of love as a symbol of victory but draws a constant mockery of it as sadistic whose 'triumph' rests only in the emotion's 'failing'. The poet also believes that the emotion of male personified *love-child* is a miser in his giving and behaves aloof and detached when it comes to 'favours'. The 'virtues' are extremely mocked and questioned by the poet only due to the fact that Wroth attempts to portray the emotional, psychological trauma that one goes through the process of making love and being in love. The poet asserts the fact that love is a painful affair and love is like a child whose behaviour causes pain and the sentiment towards the child's innocence and sweetness will earn the glory in the end. Therefore, the poet calls attention to certain ignored dark side of love.

In the final stanza of the poem, Wroth gets too critical of the virtues of the love and the poem does not sound any pleasant song but a painful song of being defeated by him, the child. The poet compares love to delicate and short lived 'features' of a bird in its strength and loyalty to her; the bird or the emotion. Wroth also alleges a cruel nature in love as she hyperbolically declares 'wolves' are 'no fiercer in their preying' who may cause less pain to the pray but the love causes the most pain to the love or the relation or the poet. Hence, Wroth uses imperative lines with the verbs 'leave' and 'seek' to show her firm conviction and caution in submitting oneself to the sentiment and soft emotion of love before falling prey to it.

In conclusion , Wroth claims that the emotion of love behaves like a child and possess all illogical and deceptive traits that are never possible to understand as they are unpredictable. She crafts a sarcastic and negative tone in the poem to depict the virtues of love in her Song.

Word Count: 839

3 PASSION by Kathleen Raine

IGCSE Exam Style Questions:

1. Explore how Raine vividly conveys her fears and hopes in the poem *Passion*.

   OR

2. Explore how Raine strikingly conveys the power of nature in the poem *Passion*.

   OR

3. Explore in what ways Raine vividly conveys her desire for a new world in the poem *Passion*.

   OR

4. How does Raine powerfully conveys her powerful feelings in the poem *Passion?*

Model Response: A Grade

Explore how Raine vividly conveys her fears and hopes in the poem Passion.

The poem, Passion, conveys Raine's intense emotion of love and desire for a new world. The poem brings forth speaker's fears from being heartbroken situation in the first three tercets and her hopes for a new life awakened by the nature in the last five tercets. This clear shift in the setting and tone of the poem conveys poet's fears and hopes. Abandoned by human companionship and love, Raine desperately searches for a hope in the nature; the fears leave her and she is embraced by the love of God-the nature.

The poem, Passion, opens on a startling note of poet's melancholic state of mind; conveying clear fears of abandonment by someone she loves the most. The juxtaposition between 'Full of desire' and 'wounding' in the opening line expresses her disappointment and heartbroken situation. She does 'lay' waiting but fails to receive the 'voice' of her love 'to speak' and feel hopeful 'through the mute telephone'. The oxymoron , 'mute telephone' conveys her waiting patiently to endless time that makes her feel fearful and weaker so she craves for certain peace in life. Therefore, the readers experience her loneliness and her longing for someone who never turns up to give her hopes and love her.

In the first tercet of the poem, the readers notice that the poet's agony and heart break is caused more due to lack of 'tranquillity' in her 'soul' than by 'the longed voice' that she never gets to hear. The poet deeply senses pain when the 'cloud ship' in 'the sky' sails 'without' her. The idea of 'sailing' conveys her expectations of life journey together with her love whose 'voice' becomes 'mute'. A note of sorrow emerges as she desires more from human love experiencing certain 'mortal death' and 'heart break' situation with a 'well known' person. The poet observes 'each tree possessing' the calmness and peace that she lacks in her soul as the love is never in the reach for her. When the poet looks inside herself, she does not feel the peace but finds it outside in the nature. Therefore, she feels fears not being embraced by the love of God in the form of nature.

The third tercet in Passion, the poet conveys the failure of reconciliation with her love. The poet attempts to establish her cordial relationship in 'the language' she 'knew best' but she fails to convince and win her love back. The poet uses metaphor of 'the savage conches' to depict the separation between herself and the protection of love-the shell. The poet's 'human speech' fails to win back her love spoken in the best form of 'Homer's ghosts'; a literary allusion which reveals the genuine attempts of her to persuade her love through speeches. In the end, the speaker loses her ability to speak and her 'body' grows weak. The hyperbole of failure conveys speaker's inability to change the mind of her lover. Thereof, the poet vividly conveys the fears of human separation and unattained love and lack of peace.

On the other hand, the speaker enormously conveys her hopes in the nature and celestial creations in the sky. The sudden shift from the human setting to natural setting brings the tone of positivity in the poem. The personified 'sky' reassures the speaker's 'soul' affirming that she has 'what you desire'. The poet attempts to create a relationship between human life and the nature around us. The speaker conveys that the nature has the healing power and it drives away the crippled emotions in human life. She feels 'love' in her 'heart' for the first time in watching the beauty of 'clouds, winds, starts and ever moving seas'. The multiple images enrich the beauty of the poem as well as the heart of the speaker. Hence, The speaker realises that humans 'are born' with nature which is the reality and truth in the world.

In the sixth tercet of the poem, the symbol of God in the form of sky provides the speaker with two options to live and embrace love. The imperative 'Lift up your heart' indicates that God's direct conversation in a 'language clear'. The adverb 'again' suggests a fresh beginning of her life with an option of breathing 'the living air' but not to live with 'fear in the tomb'. The symbol, tomb, depicts the fears of death in silence the speaker experienced with 'mute telephone' in the first verse of the poem. Finally, the readers feel relieved when the speaker is offered entire new 'world' with a 'share' of natural world of 'flowers' and animal world of 'tiger'. Thus, the speaker feels hopeful from the God's creations; the nature which is above human love.

Soon after the speaker receives hopes and experiences a new beginning in life witnessing entirely a new world. The poet now sees 'every visible substance' in the world around her being immortal. The theme of immortality emerges in the poem with the permanence of nature. The speaker begins to experience a new world with 'holy fire of passion'. Though the poet beings to see holiness and rejoice with her hopes returned, she desires for a new 'world'; creating certain ambiguity in the poem. The biblical allusion 'judgment day' suggests that there comes a new beginning of the world. The new beginning becomes definitive idea after the poet expects it when 'the war ends' and conflict in the world 'rolls away'. The readers understand that the speaker attempts to transfer her newly attained hope and love to the entire world with 'light and eternity'. Therefore, the poet conveys her hopes for herself as well as the world.

In conclusion, Raine vividly conveys that the human life is full of pain and agony without true love but she believes that these crippled emotions of pain can be driven away by the God's love -the nature and celestial creations which are holy. In a way, she places God's love above human love establishing a relationship between the human and nature for a tranquil life.

Word Count: 1002

4 LOVE (III) by George Herbert

IGCSE Exam Style Questions:

1. Explore how Gorge Herbert vividly conveys the meaning of love through the dramatic dialogue between the speaker and the Love in the poem.

   OR

2. How does George Herbert vividly portray the relationship between the speaker and the Lord in the poem *Love (III)?*

   OR

3. Explore the ways in which George Herbert strikingly creates feelings of guilt in the poem *Love(III)*.

   OR

4. Explore how George Herbert vividly presents the Lord as symbol of love in the poem *Love (III)*.

   OR

5. Explore how George Herbert vividly portrays the virtues/attributes
    of the Lord in the poem *Love (III)*.

Model Response: A Grade

*Explore how Gorge Herbert vividly conveys the meaning of love through the dramatic
dialogue between the speaker and the Love in the poem.*

In the poem, Love(III) by George Herbert, readers intriguingly witness a
dramatic dialogue between speaker and the personified character of Love
that speaks parallel to the status of Omnipotent. It is interesting to note that
the meaning of Love is implicitly embedded in the poem, which is absolute
wonder for the poet, as he believes that it is not even imaginable aspect for
him to meet Love, the image of the Lord. There are instances where Love
embraces the speaker though he is reluctant to join the Lord for a meal with
Him.

In treatment, the poet describes the moment of time, where the speaker
meets the Lord, as unimaginable and magnificent. The delightful moment
spent with Love is truly wonderful for the poet in the poem. The poet
conveys that the gesture of God to meet the poet is defined as gesture of
Love. The poet seems humbled when 'Love' greets him and 'welcome' to
'eat' with him. The poet alludes the readers to imagine the communion of
'Lord' with his disciples. It is the joy of touch by the Lord when He takes
the poet's 'hand'. The poet is seen as overwhelmed to observe Lord's
abundant Love despite all his shortcomings. In this manner, the poet
portrays the gesture of Lord coming forward as gesture of showing Love.

To convey the meaning of Love, the poet takes up such a subject of impossibility to meet the Lord. The meeting between mortal and immortal becomes the subject of Love where **He** is portrayed as forgiving. The poet believes that the forgiving nature is nothing but 'Love'. The speaker is completely with a belief that he is bound to meet 'dust' as a mortal and 'sin' on this planet. However, Lord addresses the speaker as 'dear' twice and forgives him without request. The repetition of the word 'dear' testifies His love and it richly reinforces the fact that God can only show Love and nothing else. Therefore, Lord becomes the symbol of Love towards the end of the poem. This gesture of forgiveness is described as Love in the poem.

The poet makes a deal of treatment of contradictions in the poem to highlight the weaknesses of man and greatness of the Lord. Despite the fact that the speaker announces and accepts that he is 'guilty', 'unkind', and 'ungrateful', the Lord 'draws 'nearer' so positively to put the speakers at ease. This attitude of Lord becomes heavy on the part of the speaker to accept His love. The diction chosen for the speaker such as 'guilty, dust, and sin' make a contradiction to the attributes of Lord, such as 'sweetly', 'My dear' and 'smiling'. These contradictions creates a point for the readers and the Lord wins the heart of the speaker through His Love.

In the next context, the readers wonder to note that the virtues of Lord spread the idea of love when He takes all the 'blame' of the speaker and embraces him despite being a sinner and guilty of 'dust'. The idea of acceptance by Lord makes the poem more lovable. The theme of 'Love' between the Host who wishes to 'serve' and the guest who hesitates be 'worthy' in front of Lord's stature intrigues the readers. It becomes honour for the speaker to go 'where' it is understood as heaven due to Lord's presence. It is interesting to note that the poet employs religious allusion to imply that 'where' is nothing but hell. Therefore, the idea of hell is disposed and the idea of 'Love' and compassion of Lord is magnified in the poem.

The poem is composed through narrative form in the first stanza and a dramatic dialogue in the second and third stanza. Therefore, the conversation between Love and the poet becomes sweet moment and the moment of Love. In this conversation, Love wins the heart of the poet by being compassionate, caring and welcoming. The 'quick-eyed Love' observes the hesitation felt by the poet, which explains how caring Lord is. Lord is always 'smiling' in His replies to the poet and smile becomes the symbol of compassion and acceptance of the guilty. Ultimately, the Lord takes the 'blame' which describes the crucifixion of God in the poem, an allusion makes the way into the poem to describe the Lord's virtues and attributes of Love.

On the other hand, it is exciting for the readers to identify the relationship between the speaker and the Lord in the poem, where a numerous ways of relationships are identified within the dramatic dialogue form. In each of these, there is only the Love that is understood by the readers. In the first place, He is the Love and poet is the loved. Second, poet is described as sinner and Lord as redeemer who forgives; another note of love for the poet. Third, the poet is the victim but in the safe hands of saviour. Fourth, it the conversation between Omnipotent and insignificant speaker makes it special moment. In all these ways, Lord is presented to only show Love and the speaker receives it from the God.

In conclusion, the poem Love is made absolutely special with the dialogue between a mere man and powerful God but loving. The poet's efforts seem to be that God is symbol of love that can only render love and nothing else whereas the speaker is portrayed as hesitant of his guilt and sin. In the end, Love wins the heart of the speaker to join the Lord.

Word Count: 917

5 *LOVERS' INFINITENESS* by John Donne

IGCSE Exam Style Questions:

1. Explore how John Donne intriguingly conveys his arguments about his love and the beloved in the poem *Lovers' Infiniteness*.

   OR

2. How does John Done vividly express his love in the manner of a debate in *Lovers' Infiniteness*?

   OR

3. Explore how John Done strikingly develops the debate of reconciliation in the poem *Lovers' Infiniteness*.

   OR

4. Explore the ways in which John Done creates vivid images and intriguing diction of love in *Lovers' Infiniteness*.

   OR

5. Explore how Donne effectively uses the dramatic monologue form in the poem Lovers' Infiniteness.

OR

6. How does John Done make the feelings of the speaker so vivid in *Lovers' Infiniteness*?

OR

7. How does the poet vividly convey feelings about love either in Lovers' Infiniteness (by John Donne) or Heart and Mind (by Edith Sitwell)? (Note: Combination questions are frequent in IGCSE board examinations)

Model Response: A Grade

Explore how John Donne intriguingly conveys his arguments about his love and the beloved in the poem Lovers' Infiniteness.

In the beginning of the poem *Lover's Infiniteness*, John Donne develops an irrational debate with his lady love though reasonable; who seem not to share her infinite love for him. The poet intriguingly presents three fold appeal and debate to claim his love; being confident to get all the love from his lover. The poet directly addresses the lover and makes his assertions to plead for infinite love. It is ironical on the part of the speaker who questions the lover for all the love of her and answers himself that he cannot have it; yet slates a compromise in the end of the poem.

In a tone of disappointment, the poem begins with a clause as a lawyer's reasoning and more of a debater softly seeking love from the beloved. The introduction of the grammatical clause 'If yet I have not' asserts that the poet knows the reply but in a dilemma asking for assurance from the lover. The negative self-reply that he cannot 'have it all' contradicts all the hope of the poet. The readers empathise with the poet to note his efforts of 'sighs and 'tears' that fall for 'love'. The poet's diction makes the reader wonder how the poet considers the play of love as a business deal for which he 'spent' all his 'sighs, tears, oaths and letters'; all his 'treasure' to 'purchase' love. Thereof, the debate runs into an interesting manner of self-debate.

In the middle of the first stanza, the poet's impatience is noticeable and he gives up his efforts to wait and seek the love. He imagines he has competitors in the pursuit of love. The poet feels that all the 'bargain made' is 'due' to him. He disapproves the 'partial love' as 'gift' for him and demands 'others' should not have space for her love. The manner in which the poet employs repetition as in the salutation of an informal letter 'Dear' hints that he is still hopeful of her love but the stanza closes on the note of not having her love or expresses his disinterest to have it only 'all' but not any part of her love. Thus, the poem interestingly develops into a debate in writing form of a letter.

As the poem progresses, the debate of poet turns too far-fetched and rational. Proudly, he claims that he is the first one who laid the seed of love in her heart. Quite interestingly, he states that the lover begins to 'grow new love by other men' and he does not approve of it and demands that he 'should have it all'. The merchandise diction of 'outbid' again reaffirms the fact how the poet looks at the 'stock of love'. The natural imagery of 'ground' presents a new thought in the readers' mind how the poet makes it logical that whatever 'grows' in the heart of the lover is his. The repetition of 'sighs, oaths, and letters' indicate that the poet has no further intention to 'bid' for her love as he has 'new fears' of 'other men' may create. Thus, the poet's apprehension and treatment of love with the diction of business makes it interesting for the readers.

In the last stanza of the poem, the poet fears new growth of love. Though he expresses his apprehensions, he does not feel that he will be able take the new love as he already received it in entirety then. The indication of 'new growth' and 'new rewards' suggests that the poet does not want the lover to receive attention from anyone except him to have all the love from her. Thereby, he presents himself as an obsessed admirer of her. It also portrays the possessive nature of the poet who seems obsessed to have 'it all'. The repetition of 'it all' seven times in the poem reiterates the point that the poet does not want except 'all love' and wishes his 'love' should not 'admit love' everyday. It opens the debate wide and open who or what the 'new love' is. Therefore, the poets argument continues for infinite love.

In a complete twist in the debate by the poet, he intriguingly slates a compromise deal as he does not see an end to his debate at all. He cleverly proposes a new deal which explains that instead of exchange of love the poet wishes to bind the hearts into one. This deal is brought up due his failure to understand how the 'love's riddles are' too complex to understand. His compromises are understandable when he treats the deal as 'more liberal', a 'way, that is more convenient to him than to the beloved.

He surprises the readers in the last two lines concluding the mutual but one-sided understanding can be achieved by not 'changing the hearts' but only to 'join them' so that all the love in both the hearts cannot be measured. This act of joining the hearts seems more of psychological and symbolical union of the poet with her and his compromise at the end of the poem.

In the end of the poem, the poet attempts to resolve the argument and find an intermediate solution of his own argument with his beloved. It seems to be a comprise that the poet attempts to bring between him and his lover. He requests her to join the hearts to be one, which is all that the poet wishes to have for all. The antithesis suggests the poet's claims the opposite though the reader does not understand what convinced the poet. Definitely, the poem ends on a note of ambiguity of how the poet reaches out a solution of his own for a debate he began; where the beloved does not take part at all.

Word Count: 956

6 *SHE WAS A PHANTOM OF DELIGHT*
by William Wordsworth

IGCSE Exam Style Questions:

1. Explore how Wordsworth vividly portrays a perfect Woman in the poem *She was a Phantom of Delight*.

   OR

2. Explore the ways in which Wordsworth vividly portrays a transition of his Woman in the poem *She was a Phantom of Delight*.

   OR

3. What does Wordsworth make you feel about the Woman in the poem *She was a Phantom of Delight*?

   OR

4. Explore how the poet vividly portrays the delight of three moments/phases of love in the poem *She was a Phantom of Delight*

   OR

5. Explore in detail how Wordsworth memorably conveys his delight in the poem *She was a Phantom of Delight*.

OR

6. Explore how the poet's words vividly portray the emotion of being in love in the poem *She was a Phantom of Delight*.

OR

7. Explore how Wordsworth seeks delight from the spirit of his woman in the poem *She was a Phantom of Delight*.

Model Response: A Grade

Explore how Wordsworth vividly portrays a perfect Woman in the poem She was a Phantom of Delight.

In the poem *She was a Phantom of Delight*, William Wordsworth memorably portrays a perfect Woman who transforms from her quality of being a spirit. From the moment of his first sight, she changes to a completely different woman when seen from a closer and serene eye of the poet. The poet exuberantly presents the moments of joy to watch her at different distances and different states of observation. The woman transforms from a mere image of joy to watch to a perfect Woman. The poet makes it memorable with the contrast presented of the perfect woman who is presented as a phantom at the beginning of the poem.

The poet begins the poem to portray the beauty of the lady and contradictory nature of the lady's looks that take away the breath of the poet at first sight. At the time of meeting her for the first time, the moment becomes a precious one for him to enjoy. Her apprearance makes the moment unbelieavalbe and glowing for him. When the poet meets the women first, she 'gleamed upon' him in the first 'singht'. The appearance of her makes the 'moment' so 'lovely' for him to enjoy her unearthly beauty. The readers apprehend that poet calls her 'apparition' and feels her like a spirit as the poet fails to forget the perfect Woman he meets. Interestingly, the poet highlights how she is beautiful and attarctive like an ornament but disturbing like a spirit for him.

The poet significantly highlights that the woman of his fascination is more beautiful than the nature itself as he describes her as a crature or spirit made of all the natural elements that the day and darkness show to the world. The poet makes a hyperbolic description of the women and attributes that she is made of several natural elements such as 'stars' in hers eyes, her 'hair' of 'dusky' nautre and all her personality is shaped by 'Twilight' and the season of 'may-time' and the delightful 'dawn'. All this description peppers the poem as an exaggeration of her beauty but the poet experiences the joy to watch her so perfect for his eyes. Ultimately, he falls in love with her perfect personlaity because of the nature and its beauty that she holds in her shape.

In the second stanza, when he begins to see his love in a closer view, the poet startles the readers that he enjoys so many happy moments with the perfect woman but also he brings an idea that they do have certain meloncholic moments too. The poet makes the readers jeolous of his romatic life when he conveys his romance with his 'kisses' and love' that makes them so close and bond well in life. This romantic description indicates the stong bond of understanding and knowing each other. However, he uses oxymoron of two contrary emotions in the poem where he hints that they also have 'tears' and 'blame' in their relation. It is not just sadness but they also 'praise' each other for their attributes and 'smile' and enjoy each other's company. In brief, the poet brings forth both happy moments and sad moments in their life though he claims thier relation as perfect with a perfect woman.

In the last stanza of the poem, the poet shows greater admiration for the perfect woman and praises her skills or virtues as woman to be impressive to any eye. The poet list several virtures of her to bring the impact to the readers for more admiration. To begin with, the poet likes her for her quality to be very careful in every 'breath' and how she is 'thoughtful' every moment. He also declares that she has the capacity to face hardships in life and how she is made of the virtue of 'endurance'. The poet also praises her for her 'forsight' and 'temperate will' and power to tackle everything in his life in the household activities. Finally, he thinks that she is full of great qualities as a human being and so he declares her a PERFECT woman.

Wordsworth memorably illustrates the captivatating effect of the woman on him and adores her from the very first sight of the sun light on this planet. Though readers noitce a contradicting description of her as a ' phantom of delight', the poet extrapolates from the last stanza that she possess the power of transforming herself to breathtaking beauty with true virtues to be a perfect woman for him. The aura of her presence almost transforms poet's home a heaven with a bright light of 'Dawn' of 'May time' from her personality. Her 'dancing shape' and 'image' are so delightful that it does not make him feel her presence rather 'haunts' him and 'startles' his loss of self. Thus, the poet fails to resist her immsense beauty and flawless personlality of a perfect Woman.

In brief, the poem presents contrasts yet qualifies the woman to be a perfect lady for the poet's eyes. The impact of her on him seems more delightful than her appearance to be an apparition or the spirit to cause fear. The perfect Woman truly stands impeccable with her virtures being so robust in the last stanza.

WORD COUNT: 869

7 *TIGER IN THE MENAGERIE* by Emma Jones

IGCSE Exam Style Questions:

1. Explore how Jones vividly portrays the captivity of the tiger in the poem *Tiger in the Menagerie.*

    OR

2. Explore how Jones creates striking images in the poem *Tiger in the Menagerie.*

    OR

3. Explore how Jones vividly portrays the relationship between the tiger and the menagerie in the poem *Tiger in the Menagerie.*

    OR

4. Explore the ways in which Jones vividly portrays beauty and power of the tiger in the poem *Tiger in the Menagerie.*

OR

5. In what ways does Jones vividly portrays the tiger in the poem *Tiger in the Menagerie ?*

Model Response: A Grade

Explore how Jones vividly portrays the captivity of the tiger in the poem Tiger in the Menagerie.

In the poem Tiger in the Menagerie, Jones vividly portrays tiger's beauty, captivity, power and loss of freedom. Jones intriguingly orients the readers with symbolism of tiger to its instincts of violence and wildness and untamed nature in captivity. Not only the poet wonders at the beauty of the tiger conveying through her pictorial description but also she deliberates on human interference in the freedom and life of tiger.

Though the poem opens with abruptness of disarray for tiger's entrance into the menagerie, Jones understandably wonders , in the second line of the poem, at the beauty and splendid sight of the tiger's 'too flash' of its beauty creating radiance all around. The opulent colour of amber on tiger draws chromatic effect as 'too blue' in the menagerie amid other birds; dominating its physical magnificence and weakening their aura before its grand appearance. The poet draws a simile and compares with hyperbolic effect of tiger's beauty to that of a 'painting' which is too much' picturesque and exquisite to view. The structure of the poem in tercets and couplets explicitly resembles the beautiful and irregular stripes on the tiger's hide. The poet paints the tiger's body in the structure of the poem on surface level. Therefore, the poet vividly transforms her wonder and awe to the readers through her portrayal of tiger's grand sight in the menagerie.

In the second tercet of the poem, Jones abruptly loses her wonder and depicts the captivity and enslavement forced on it by human interference; which 'No one could say' to the poet's orientation and awakenedness. The readers suddenly witness the tiger in 'the cage' symbolising tiger's loss of freedom and enslavement. The poet creates pity for tiger's 'time' in solitude and the confusion created in 'those eyes' until 'so long' in 'the night'. The tiger ponders on its predicament in 'the cage' where 'the bars of the cage' and 'the stripes of the tiger' are personified to engage in understanding their displacement. Due to their resemblance, they try to understand the reason behind their displacement. The pity, in the readers, awakens when 'it was time for those eyes to rock shut'; which is the indication of their failure to learn why they resemble same creating confusion. In fact, the poet points out that the confusion indicates tiger's frequent displacement and captivity; which comes to surface when the poet does not get answers on 'how the tiger got into' and ' how the tiger got out' of the menagerie. The use of inverse metaphor of 'bars and stripes' caused due to inflicting pain though lashing also conveys the chaos created for tiger in the menagerie. Therefore, the poet believes that the menagerie is symbolic of tiger's loss of freedom and enslavement which draws readers' sympathy for its plight at nights.

In the third tercet, the poet parades the readers along the tiger to convey the tiger's desire for freedom through the expression of tiger's 'dreams'. The dreams of tiger are conveyed through 'bars' and stripes' which 'walked together...so long' to indicate the desire for a longevity of freedom. The 'colonnade' symbolises freedom not only for the fact that it does not confine the tiger's movement in any possible side and roof in its structure but also its symbolic representation of human liberty which tiger craves for in the form of 'fretwork'. Though the fretwork creates an image of an ornamental pattern yet it conveys the wild and feral that the tiger need to reach in the vastness of freedom; as expressed in the metaphor of 'Indian main'. The poet alludes the 'Indian main' to draw parallelism between vastness of the ocean and scope of its dream walk. Therefore, the dream walk endorses tiger's desire for freedom into the wild from menagerie but it vanishes when the 'sun' rises.

In fourth tercet, Jones brings forth the true nature and impact of tiger's presence. The poet depicts tiger's violence and power through its 'too bare' and wild nature to cause fears in its crude form but 'too bright' conveys tiger's swiftness and quickness in the small space for its movements in the menagerie. The readers observe the tiger's power in letting loose itself in the line, 'how the tiger got out in the menagerie'. Though 'No one could say' and enlighten the poet or the readers, it is evident to pursue that tiger's entry into and exit from the menagerie does show external control enforced on it and its power to let loose respectively. Hence, The poet depicts menagerie as a collective domain of captive animals and conveys the fears experienced by them as 'it would say 'tiger' to draw the idea of fears and menace caused on its let loose situation from the wild.

In the last tercet of the poem, Jones creates vivid image of beautiful patterns of birds which contradicts the violence created on tiger's entry 'inside to wait' in the 'aviary'. The fears among the birds can be heard in 'aviary's heart beat' and compulsion to 'lock its doors'. These attempts of locking aviary and 'heart beat' caused clearly indicates the fact that violence resonates 'when tiger came inside the aviary'. On contrast, Jones creates wonderful image of rows of rising birds to paint a pattern of birds flying in the aviary. Poet's motive to end the poem on the note of violence draws the meaning to advocate that the natural instinct of wildness and aggression of the tiger cannot establish a relationship with menagerie which is a symbol of control. The poet attempts to conclude with an idea that human nature verses animal nature draws closeness of civility and wildness in both.

In conclusion, Jones vividly portrays different facets of tiger being in the menagerie. The poet extrapolates tiger's sight in the menagerie, its beauty, its predicament, its relationship with menagerie, and violence to advocate freedom and liberty for the tiger in the wild but not in the menagerie.

Word Count: 970

8 *LION HEART* by Amandan Chong

IGCSE Exam Style Questions:

1. In what ways Amanda Chong vividly portrays the spirit of mythical beast/legendary icon in the poem *lion heart*.

    OR

2. How does Chong strikingly convey the power of lion in the poem *lion heart*?

    OR

3. Explore how the poets' words create striking pictures (images) of the lion and its presence in the poem *lion heart*?

    OR

4. Explore how the poet powerfully conveys transformation of the land in the poem *lion heart*.

    OR

5. Explore how Chong powerfully expresses her exuberance in presenting the mythical figure in the poem *lion heart*.

Model Response: A Grade

In what ways Amanda Chong vividly portrays the spirit of mythical beast/ legendary icon in the poem lion heart.

In the poem *lion heart* Amanda Chong strikingly portrays the lion as a power and spirit that create a positive aura and atmosphere on the island nation. The description of the arrival of the lion in the opening of the poem is sheer indication of its power and spirit that it spreads across the shores of the land. The physical features of the beast are portrayed with immense brightness and strength to show so much of lion's positive influence on the shore. Though it is a mythical beast, the poet's exuberant tone transforms the lion as a legendary figure for the nation or a histroical icon; which suggests the significance of the spirit that it spreads for the people here.

Amanda Chong megestically portrays the grand arrival of the lion from the sea. The glittering description of the lion speaks itself the spirit that it brings to the land. The poet's exuberance is evident when she uses the second person pronoun 'You' for it originates from the 'sea'. The respectable addressing indicates the power and spirit it brought over the 'ridding crests' on the waves of the 'sea'. The power of the lion is witnessed when the 'water' is 'whipped the first breath' from its 'lungs'. These actions suggest its transformation from a sea creature to be a spirit of progress and wealth for the island nation's humble beginnings. Thereof, the lion's arrival is more significant for a transformed island that is portrayed in the stanzas later.

Chong powerfully illustrastes the evolution of the mythical beast from a sea-lion to famously known spirit of Merlion that 'embraced them' who 'embraced the land' from far off places to signify integrity of the state. The description of the power of the lion through the phrases 'your hand' 'summoned' indicate the very spirit it has over 'the land' for a new world created. The poet signifies the fact that it is the beast's spirit that 'sunk' strong 'roots' of wealth, progress, integrity and positivity in its presence over the 'surface' of this island. Thus, the poet memorably recollects the origins of the beast and its permanence in the hearts of the people here.

In the second stanza of the poem, Chong entirely dedicates her exuberance in the description of lion's physical strength, power and spirit. The readers get a feeling that it is the beast's strength that brought power to the land as it 'conquered the shore' and turned a mere fishing island village into a stronger, stable and prosperous 'ivory coast' for its people. The metaphorical resemblance of the lion to be 'a prince' undercurrently states the fact how its 'heart thumped' for a prosperous and wealthy change but a humbel one. Chong powerfully draws parallel between the strenght of the nation today and the lion's power as kingly and projects as spirit for its people.

Chong powerfully presents the lion as a symbol of national pride ,spirit and unity. These attributes of the land strongly upholds the spirit of brotherhood; where the land is culturally diverse in its 'roots'. The spirit and power of the land seem to have been drawn from the 'roar' and 'call' and 'squall' from the 'golden sheen'. The richness of the place equals the richness of lion's 'eyes' that 'flicker'; in brignt 'emarald'. Finally, the poet joys the beast's interest when 'settled' on its 'back on fluent haunches' that indicate its presence being made so strongly on the land forever.

The poet strongly emphasises the role of the beast in nation building. Chong undercurrently presents the fact how the lion guides the people through its spirit. Intriguingly, the poet reminds how the lion elevates the island from its simple 'oceanice origins' to the hights of 'skyscrapers'. The symbolic representation of skyscrapers that 'rise' from 'trees' suggest that the land evolved from nature's gift of 'trees' and 'green' to 'higher' status in the world's eye. In the process, the poet not only reminds the readers of land's 'oceanic origins' but also its success stroy of trade by 'the sea's pulmonary' for 'Centuries' till today. To mark this prosperity, Chong rests the glory be to the spirit of the mythical beast; a lion with a 'heart' that is so big to be called Merlioin of Singapore today.

In the last three short stanzas and couplet, Chong strongly reminds the nation of its original 'self ' and its 'raw lion heart' that holds the spirit of the people here. She urges readres to remember its culture through the use of weaponry 'keris' and 'iron lightning'. Its 'double-edged' quality is nothing but its spirit that drives them towards positivity and its wealth that shapes the 'red tapestry' flutter so hight in the 'sky' with 'five stars' in it. She does not want to leave a chance for the people to forget their origins and spirit that runs in their 'pulmonary'. The repetition of 'You' not only refer to the lion but also the nation and its people and its spirit. Thereofore, the poem narrates a wonderful story behind the success of the island nation; Singapore.

In conclusion, the poem *lion heart* doest not only speak of the lion but also more of its spirit and its people. The poet urges readers to note that it is the spirit that makes difference to its people and the land but not its wealth and prosperity today. Gently, she also draws the culutre and history of the land in her portrayal of the island village's transformation.

WORD COUNT: 913

9 *HEART AND MIND* by Edith Sitwell

IGCSE Exam Style Questions:

1. Explore how Sitwell powerfully portrays the despair (of love) in the poem *Heart and Mind*.

   OR

2. In what ways Sitwell intriguingly portrays the correlation between the heart and the mind in the poem.

   OR

3. How does Sitwell effectively use the dramatic monologue form in the poem *Heart and Mind*.

   OR

4. Explore how Sitwell vividly portrays the idea of glory in the poem *Heart and Mind*.

Model Response: A Grade

In what ways Sitwell intriguingly portrays the correlation between the heart and the mind in the poem.

The poem Heart and Mind intriguingly presents Sitwell's observations of life and its glorious ideas of immortality despite the inevitable death and despair of love associated with it. The poet employs three dramatic monologues and engages the readers in the dialogues of the Lion, the Skeleton and the Sun with the passive listeners , the Lioness, the readers and the Moon respectively. In these intriguing monologues, the poet brings forth the ideas of eternity of time and heart, consciousness, despair of love and philosophical lines of immortality. The poet conveys the correlation between the heart and the mind in each monologue and the poem turns philosophical at the end.

In the first monologue, the poet introduces a hypothetical situation where the Lion's mind proposes the idea of death that conveys mortality but the Lion's heart attempts to defeat it by bringing out the idea of immortality after life. The passive listener, the Lioness, is told the imaginative situation 'When you are amber dust-' to foresee the death. The Biblical allusion 'dust' conveys the idea of death when there is no 'raging fire' in their life to live with immense enthusiasm. The Lion expresses that the 'liking' does die before death and there remains only the 'lust'. Despite the fact that mortality is associated with life as the mind of the Lion foresees well before, however he disposes it with his philosophy of immortality in the heart. Therefore, the Lion indulges in a more imaginative future to bring his heart and idea of immortality after death despite despair of love in life.

On contrast to the idea of death, the Lion shows more unfailing faith in immortality and glory of past life's strength. The Lion urges the Lioness to 'remember' how the growth of their life takes way into 'flowering of amber blood and bone'. The Lion emphasises the fact that it is the strength in 'the rippling bright muscles' that signify their life and glory in life to remember before death as they are the most powerful in the jungles. The repetition of 'Remember' and comparison of their strength to the ripples in 'sea' convey the undying faith in the heart of the Lion which believes in immortality after life. He expresses a wonderful feeling in delicate imagery of 'the rose' in the 'bright paws' when their youth peaks to the best form. The poet creates a connection between the heart and mind which become 'one' only with 'the heart' meeting the death. Therefore, the poet portrays a relationship between the heart and the mind.

In the monologue of Skeleton, Sitwell immortalises time before the Lion's thoughts whose broodings of glory of past appears to be immortal though not in trueness. The symbol of death 'Skeleton' rightly conveys that the powerful 'tawny body of Lion' burns to 'dust' in the passage of time. Further in the poem, she asserts the fact that 'The great gold planet' stands as a symbol of 'Time' which emerges 'more powerful' before 'all that grows or leaps'. The poet builds an idea that everything that takes birth and lives on the planet must meet the dust. The 'sands' form the image of 'mourning heat of the sun' in the stanza which implies the time as immortal before 'all' on the planet and nothing strong or weak remains but is 'consumed' in the passage of time. Thereof, the poet refutes the lines from the heart of the

Loin to the Lioness about the past glory; conveying the reciprocation between heart and mind deems disoriented being together in one domain of physical body of the living.

In more narrative lines from the Greek mythology, Sitwell meditates sharply and conveys that the heart over powers the mind though the mind occupies itself in more logical and reasoned thoughts. Presenting the love tales of ' Hercules and Samson', the poet believes that both Greek heroes were betrayed in love despite warnings from mind. Samson's mind suspects Delilah and resists the temptation of inducing her but the 'heart' of Samson and its sentiment and love for Delilah 'consumed' him and 'the mind'. The mind smells the truth of possible danger that brings his fall. His blindness to love and belief in himself 'as strong as pillars of seas' kills him eventually as with the story of Hercules who does fall for Deianira's obsession for his love. Hercules' weakness for woman's love reflects ' the flames of the heart' more powerful than mind's truth and reality. In the end, 'the mind' evolves as only 'a foolish wind' before the sentiments and emotions of the heart. Hence, the poet draws on a sound correlation between the hearts and mind through the analogy of Greek tales.

In the dramatic monologue between the Sun and the Moon which are the symbols of masculine and feminine energy, Sitwell emphatically states the despair of their 'love'. The Sun despairs that 'the Moon' hangs as a 'lonely white crone' in the end of their love life; unable to meet forever separated by distance between heart and mind. 'The Sun' declares himself as 'a dead King'. It depicts his power in 'golden armour' remains powerless ' in a dark wood'. The poet claims that the Sun's power fails to reach earth's insignificant forests which equal his failure to be with his 'love'. They 'never' come together 'till Time is done' that contradicts their love's triumph. The poet generates the idea that the love never triumphs till 'the fire of the heart and the fire of the mind' emerge as 'one' element but not two domains in the body.

In conclusion, Sitwell states that the heart and the mind are two separate entities that cohabit physically in one body but never coexist in action; which distinctly evident in the three monologues. The passive listeners the Lioness and the Moon convey the acceptance with the ideas of the Lion, the Sun, Hercules and Samson whose hearts triumph failing the logic of their minds in the end. This failure proves the correlation between heart and mind a mere idea of possibility but impossible in trueness.

Word Count: 1014

10 *FOR MY GRANDMOTHER KNITTING*
by Liz Lochhead

IGCSE Exam Style Questions:

1. In what ways Lochhead vividly portrays (the memories of) the grandmother in the poem *For My Grandmother Knitting*.

    OR

2. Explore how Lochhead memorably portrays the hands of the grandmother in the poem *For My Grandmother Knitting*.

    OR

3. How does Lochhead critically convey the ideas about aging and identity in the poem *For My Grandmother Knitting?*

    OR

4. Explore how Lochhead vividly portrays the spirit of the grandmother in the poem *For My Grandmother Knitting*.

    OR

5. How does Lochhead critically convey the relationship between gradmother and grandchildren in the poem *For My Grandmother Knitting?*

OR

6. Explore how Lochead critically expresses the attitude of the grandchildren towards the grandmother in the poem *For My Grandmother Knitting.*

Model Response: A Grade

Explore how Lochhead memorably portrays the hands of the grandmother in the poem For My Grandmother Knitting.

Liz Lochhead's poem opens with a stunning and complaining words of the grandmother. In the opening line of the poem , the grandchildren are critically unappreciative of grandmother's knitting and her efforts to be an important individual in her family. She is misunderstood and made to feel that she is unimportant being in the phase of rapid aging. The shuttling of her memories between the present time and past time in the first three stanzas makes this evident that grandmother constantly remembers her glorious past with strong hands and being important member to raise the children ad help the husband.

Lochhead chooses the voice of autobiographical narration of grandmother's life in the present time and past life in the poem. The poet critically hints that the grandmother feels alienation and separation from her grandchildren and family as she chooses to call the family 'they' who 'say' nothing appreciative of her but 'You are old now'. The choice of present tense in the poem indicates her rebellion and her 'needles move' to mark her choice; remaining busy and feeling herself important. Her memories constantly take her back into the past and make her feel happy as a 'fisher-girl'. In her view, 'they' remind her old age and weak body but not her past life that raised them all. The poet seems to regret for the grandmother's state of rapid aging.

The poet strongly feels that the grandmother is constantly reminded of her weakness and old age. This act of the grandchildren forces her to fall into her sweet memories about herself as a 'master' of her life and family and 'moments' too. The sibilance of 'sure and skilful' makes her past so significant in contrast to her present life in the chair only to be 'deft and swift' with her 'hands'. The 'hands' are portrayed as symbolic of her strength when the grandmother was 'miner's wife'. The memories keep her satisfied as she only receives critical remarks from her grandchildren that she is 'not so good' and her 'grasp' is weak both physically and mentally. Thereof, the memories of the grandmother are enormously significant to encourage herself to live the rest of her life.

In the third stanza of the poem, the speaker movingly brings back her glorious days of married life as a wife and mother. The stanza forms most number of lines, twelve , that signifies the most important phase of her life as a mother of 'six' whom she 'slapped' to discipline them. The speakers seems to regret that the grandchildren are quite ignorant of how she 'slaved' for them in the important days and phase of her life and went to work bearing those 'scraped' parts on her skin for her family. It is highly pitiful to note that her 'hard work' is not recognised now. In addition, the speaker conveys that she enjoys to be 'bride' with 'the hand span-waist' in her husband's company. Readers get a feeling that she loved to be a wife and 'scrubbed his back' when he takes 'a tin bath' by the coal fire'. These memories haunt her when the grandchildren express their ignorance and show their attitude before her

In the fourth stanza of the poem, the poet conveys the grandmothers' wish to contribute by knitting even when she is fragile and weak in her life. The grandchildren fail to reckon her emotions to feel important and to feel engaged with her life rather do nothing and be idle. The speaker wishes to be intimate with them when 'they' wear 'scarves and cardigans' but 'they' do not appreciate and respond that they 'have too much already...more than they can wear.'. It is regretful that they do not understand the knitting is her identity and engagement in her old age. Knitting also indicates her protest for them to understand her and consider it as not a waste of time. The poet creates a contrast and irony when the grandchildren remark 'grand you do too much...there is no necessity' but the same grandmother had to 'work' really 'hard' and 'it was a necessity'. Though the grandchildren utter the remarks out of love for her physical weakness, they do not completely appreciate her wish of togetherness and her need to work with hands.

In the last stanza of the poem, the voice changes from grandmother to the poet who immensely regrets the alienation and isolation experienced by her grandmother. The poet brings forth the physical damage done to her body by the family and grandchildren. The damage suggests the sacrifice she rendered and how she needs to be appreciated. The short phrases and one word expressions move the hearts of the readers to note how she turns too 'old' in the last phase of her life with 'swollen-jointed'. Red. Arthritic.' conditions in her physical body. These health conditions not only suggest her pitiful stage of life but also remind how the same body was hardworking for them once. The grandchildren seem to have 'forgotten' her contribution but not her 'hands' that swiftly work in 'patterns and rhythm'. Hence, the poet reminds the readers of her grandmothers past glory and shattered body in the present time; which needs love and care.

In the first line of fifth stanza, it is quite ironical for the readers to notice that the grandmother 'waves' to 'them' at 'her window Goodbye Sunday'. The phrase 'Goodbye Sunday' critically brings forth the truth that the goodbye is not for them but to the day that brought them to her. Ironically, 'Sunday' reminds her something but they do not remind her anything of her importance in their life. In brief, the poet expresses certain criticism about how 'old' age is not respected and cared by the grandchildren and how they ignore the sacrifices made by her. In the end, Sunday remains in her memories as a day of togetherness more than her grandchildren can provide her love and empathy that she needs.

In conclusion, the poet adopts an interesting technique of voice-switch to express the significance her grandmother through her memories and glorious days. Though there is no comparison that can be brought to make her important in the present time, the poet urges the readers to give back those memories and confidence and respect that the old need just as her grandmother. **WORD COUNT: 1052**

11 *FATHER RETURNING HOME* by Dilip Chitre

IGCSE Exam Style Questions:

1. In what ways Chitre critically conveys the isolation of the father in the poem *Father Returning Home*.

OR

2. Explore how Chitre critically portrays the father's alienation/grim existence in the poem *Father Returning Home*.

OR

3. How does Chitre movingly convey his feelings for the father in the poem *Father Returning Home?*

OR

4. Explore how Chitre uses imagery to create vivid atmosphere in the poem *Father Returning Home*.

OR

5. Explore how Chitre critically portrays life of the aged in city/suburbs in the poem *Father Returning Home*.

OR

6. In what ways does Chitre vividly create such a movingly gloomy atmosphere in the poem *Father Returning Home?*

OR

7. Explore the ways in which Chitre makes the poem *Father Returning Home* so moving for you.

OR

8. Explore the ways in which the problems of ageing are movingly conveyed by the poet either in *Father Returning Home* or *For My Grandmother Knitting*. (NOTE: Combination questions are frequent in IGCSE exams.)

Model Response: **A Grade**

Explore how Chitre movingly conveys the father's situation in the poem Father Returning Home.

In the poem Father Returns Home, Chitre movingly conveys the predicament of his father in a man-made world of metropolis and urban living style; leaving him to work in his later years of life. The poet evokes the ideas of changing society and ways of living in the cities of India. The poem not only reveals universal themes of aging, alienation from family, and predicament of an old father but also it runs the undercurrent notes of cultural elements of India in the setting of the poem and description of father. The poet deeply regrets his own father's plight and sees his extrication a difficult facet as urban life offers no emotional ties of family, affections and little comforts in the old age.

Of all circumstances surrounded the father, Chitre first creates enormous sympathy in the readers' heart for the father's aging situation. Despite the physical weakness that the father experiences, he continues to work and returns home late in the day. The father's 'eyes' are 'dimmed by age' implies not only the his vision does not help him to continue to travel or work but also his disinterest grows to head 'homeward'. The difficulty of getting home is enhanced in the poem by the setting in ' the humid monsoon night'. The gloomy imagery set for father's journey indicates the undesirable situation for the old man. The poet's description of the father in 'brown hands' covered by 'greying hairs' explicitly convey the father's aging condition which 'trembles at the sink' with 'cold water running over' him. The readers notice the fact that the father's situation craves for little comforts in his later years when he returns home. Therefore, the poet primarily conveys father's aging as a problem that is ignored by the children in a man-made world.

In an effort to denounce the metropolis life style and illusionary world created by the 'Man', Chitre portrays the solitude of the old father and gulf between him and 'His sullen children'. The poet nurses extreme remorse for the father' state of abandonment from the family. This note of irony escalates as he does remain in his 'Home' where he is not considered worthy enough 'to share Jokes and Secrets with him'. The father lacks the due regard and care from his family which can be observed in the structure of poem in one stretch or part that signifies the long life of the father leaving no special phase in old age with a couplet or quatrain in the poem. The poet uses the emotive language to convey the father's 'estrangement' is not only due to his aging but also more due to 'man-made world' where living is artificial and labouring for survival; not tied and led by love, affections, and belongingness.

Next, Chitre focuses on the mundaneness of the daily life of the father. The poet gathers certain routine of struggles on 'the late evening train' journey on his way back 'Home' to convey uneventfulness and vacuum in his life. The father encounters 'silent commuters' which implies the passive attitude of the 'suburb' dwellers who 'slide past his unseeing eyes'. For the father's eyes, city dwellers neither engage in social conversations nor they seem any interesting to him. The diction of gloomy atmosphere of the poem such as 'the late evening', 'night', 'yellow lights' and 'grey platform' marks grim life of the father. The readers witness the gloominess both in his life and physically 'dimmed' and 'unseeing eyes'. Thereof, Chitre conveys that the father struggles to find little joys of social life in the atmosphere of city life.

Further in the poem, Chitre's description of father's physical image conveys the meager life he leads and the neglect he experiences in his aging period of life. The tragic story of the old man in his 'soggy shirt and pants' indicates less protection and warmth he can get by 'his rain coat'. His journey back home in the 'sticky chappals' through the 'mud' expresses how he struggles to comfort himself from the harsh 'monsoon' weather. The poet provides clear impression that the father still works in his later years and commutes with a 'stained bag stuffed with books'. The condition of the bag which is 'falling apart' conveys the situation of his life being torn apart with inadequate economic condition for city living. This poor condition pulls strings in the hearts of the readers to think how he receives less support from his children. In addition, the father's unpleasant situation aggravates when he is 'Home again' and 'drinking weak tea' and 'Eating stale chapati'. Hence, the failure to get the company of his children at dinner conveys the lack of due care and regard he needs in his aging phase; which the poet silently watches throughout the poem leaving certain ambiguity in the poem.

In a final attempt to understand the clear picture of the father's life, Chitre looks deeper into the situation and fails to gather any meaning to his age and life. When the poet 'sees him getting off the train', he compares the life of father to 'a word dropped from a long sentence'. The poet synthesises the life of the father and thinks that the long years the father lived gathers no meaning if the old age is not lived in joys of family relationships and socialisation. The phrase 'a word' gives the effect of metaphor which expresses the loss of meaning in the sentence without it. On the other hand, 'long sentence' symbolises long life of the father. The poet conveys that the phase of old age lacks iota of meaning without care, little comforts and affections from his children or the world the man created for himself. The irony of suburb living in old age ends in 'listening' to 'the static on the radio' but not in conversations with family or urban dwellers on train. The 'dreaming' of father's 'ancestors and grandchildren' suggests his only comfort in mind to smile and rejoice a beautiful past and future; which are sweet to think rather 'contemplate' in the 'toilet' about the his condition. Thus, the poet's views convey that the life in suburbs ends in struggle and survival.

In conclusion, the poet movingly conveys the father's plight and predicament and expresses that the city life is a mere irony of man-made world of struggle and survival. He believes that Man creates a world of emptiness and pushes himself there in his old age; unaware of the fact that one must enter there one day in life. **Word Count 1087**

12 THE LOST WOMAN by Patricia Beer

IGCSE Exam Style Questions:

1. Explore the ways in which Beer movingly portrays the separation (from mother) in the poem *The Lost Woman...*

    OR

2. In what ways Beer vividly portrays the identity of the mother in the poem *The Lost Woman...*

    OR

3. Explore how Beer movingly portrays the relationship between the mother and daughter in the poem The Lost Woman...

4. In what ways Beer movingly conveys her grief in the poem The Lost Woman...

    OR

5. Explore the ways in which Beer movingly conveys the sense of loss in *The Lost Woman*...

Model Response: A Grade

Explore the ways in which Beer movingly conveys the sense of loss in The Lost Woman...

The poet, Beer, opens the elegy on an anecdotal note in The Lost Woman... The ellipsis in the title of the poem conveys volumes of grief stricken emotions untold by the poet who experiences deep sense of loss of her mother. For the poet, the mother's passing creates incalculable vacuum in her life. The poet movingly conveys immense sense of loss in her life; which the reader apprehends through the poet's memories and ideas that surface in the poem such as death, love, war, survival, bondage and identity.

Of all the six verses in the poem, the opening line of the poem not only shocks the readers with the introduction of mother's death but the poet's choice of euphemistic expression 'My mother went with no more warning' also conveys her disbelief and the grief settled in her heart for its suddenness. The uninformed departure of the mother creates 'bad pain' for the poet though not for the mother before her death. The separation from her mother after coming 'Home' creates irony as the child 'from school' witnesses the mother driven 'away' in a 'white ambulance' instead of mother waiting for her. The poet's use of imagery of 'white' implies symbol of death for the mother who is taken in a white ambulance as if it is a white linen covering her. Hence, the poet poignantly conveys her grief and loss stirring the emotions of the readers for the loss of love and bondage.

In the second verse of the poem, the passing of the mother remains heavier in the heart of the poet for she fails to get the last sight of her face. The speaker finds herself in a difficult predicament as she 'never saw her buried'. The unexpected loss and passing of the mother pushes the speaker into a kind of 'romance' or imagination to feel the mother so she calls her 'ivy-mother'. Despite the mother is no more, she lives in her memories as an ever green 'tree' and 'hops away like a rainbow'. Though certain ambiguity about the background of tree's relationship with mother is present, it is apprehensible that the poet in her imagination embraces the tree with her 'tendrils' as creepers that 'clutch' and grow over a tree for support. The use of metaphor, 'tree' for mother and 'tendrils' for the tender fingers of the child (the poet) makes the poem so moving. Hence, it is not just physical loss of the mother for the poet but the loss of emotional attachment for which she struggles and leaps into constant imagination to feel the mother.

In the third verse, the poet brings forth another anecdote which portrays the deep bondage between the poet and her mother. The poet shares sorrowful life of her mother who is 'frustrated by a dull marriage'. The dissatisfaction in married life transports the mother's love and complete engagement to the child; which conveys the deep bondage formed 'for her over the years'. 'I made a life' implies that the child provides immense emotional support for the mother. However, the readers notice that the mother 'ran a canteen through several wars' due to unhappy and unsupportive marriage but the relationship developed with the child and survival correlate in the poem. A hint of irony surfaces when the poet narrates a 'cliché' about the mother's meeting 'her match at an extra-mural class and the OU summer school'. The historical allusion of mother's survival in the war and disappointment in married life conveys the struggles of the mother. Thereof, the poet movingly conveys that the relationship shaped out of struggles and survival creates an identity for the mother to stand up and raise the poet as she hints the last verse of the poem.

The fourth verse of the poem suggests more of a feminist examination of a woman's identity and place in male-dominated world. Besides, the poet believes that 'many' men in this world whether 'a hero' or a 'poet', definitely experiences ' a lost woman' in their life ' to haunt the home'. The poet thinks that the men view the identity and the status of a woman should not 'alter' and 'grow' but remain as 'a corpse'. The metaphor of corpse to the identity of a woman reminds the readers of how the poet's mother 'never' gets the identity she deserves. The readers note that the loss of the woman is felt only when 'they need' her 'to be compensated' for domestic affairs but they 'never get to know' a woman's heart and her emotional needs. Thus, the poet deeply believes that the loss of a woman is felt in every man's life but only after her death; leaving no identity and distinctiveness when alive.

In the last two verses of the poem, the poet introduces supernatural element and eeriness to intensify 'losing' her 'lost woman'. The speaker portrays the virtues of the mother as 'benign', 'soft' and 'light' as a 'rabbit' to signify her kind and gentle personality. The speaker strongly believes that the mother, in the form of spirit, wants to 'hear how they hate themselves for losing her'. 'They' may imply the 'bland country' and her family yet 'she does not chide' them who did not care or love her when alive. In addition, the poet movingly conveys how the mother 'sacrificed too much' for the poet 'to rise above her' and grow strongly. In the end, the readers apprehend the strength the speaker gained from her sacrifices and love. Carrying mother's memories, the poet becomes 'the ghost' as she lives in her mind but 'not lost' for the her. Hence, the poet conveys that the loss of mother remains with the poet throughout her life but she feels that she never loses her emotionally.

In conclusion, the poet movingly expresses the loss of mother who raised her stronger above her but through struggles and sacrifices. The speaker conveys her grief through the use of half-rhymes without a constant flow of emotions in composition of word choices indicate poet's pain. The poet feels sorrow for the mother who never receives her true identity as a woman though not as a wife or member of the country she lived through wars running a canteen in the hard times. **Word Count: 1041**

13 COMING HOME by Owen Sheers

IGCSE Exam Style Questions:

1. Explore how Sheers critically conveys the fleeting nature of life in the poem *Coming Home.*

    OR

2. In what ways does Sheers movingly convey his thoughts and feelings for the family in the poem *Coming Home.*

    OR

3. Explore how Sheers vividly portrays the ideas of ageing and separation in the poem *Coming Home.*

    OR

4. How does Sheers critically portray the idea of mortality in the poem *Coming Home.*

OR

5. Explore how Sheers vividly portrays the futility of life in the poem *Coming Home.*

OR

6. In what ways Sheers critically conveys the reality of passing time through his family in the poem *Coming Home.*

OR

7. How does Sheers strikingly convey the contrasts between Home and being at home in the poem *Coming Home?*

Model Response: A Grade

In what ways does Sheers movingly convey his thoughts and feelings for the family in the poem Coming Home.

In the poem Coming Home, Sheers brings forth phenomenal memories on a visit to his family. At the outset of the poem, Sheers stirs the readers' emotions conveying his feelings about the mother's love. The speaker's thoughts and feelings for his mother, father and grandfather in the poem convey the ideas of aging, separation, death, fleeting nature of life and futility of life. Definitively, the poet's coming Home turns out to be ironic as he perceives discomforting and unpleasant emotions and feelings instead of a happy union with his parents and grandfather.

In the opening line of the poem, Sheer's experience with mother's warmth and love expresses certain unusualness to the readers as the poet deems the love of 'mother's hug awkward'. Though the poet's uneasiness in her embrace is shocking for the readers, it is also quite apprehensible as the maturity 'of a man' and his grown up 'body' fail to find any feeling of ease in 'the space between her open arms'. The poet conveys that the maturity of the man brings emotional separation between the son and the mother. So the poet feels that mother's embrace 'is reserved for a child' but not for a full-bodied man. The irony surfaces in the opening of the poem as the hug, which is the symbol of mother's love, results in the devoid of affection, warmth and love. Therefore, the poet movingly conveys his thoughts of separation surfacing between him and his mother as he grows into a man from being a child.

In a melancholic tone, Sheers vividly conveys his observations about his mother who begins to age. The speaker not only feels sorrow to watch his mother growing older now but also he discovers her once again in domestic routine 'in the kitchen'. The use of gerunds, 'flipping', 'patting', and 'laying' imply uneventful and routine domestic engagement of the mother. The sight of 'wrinkles' induces certain sorrow in the speaker who holds a beautiful image of the mother in his mind even as a man. However, the poet reminisces the beautiful and young mother in his mind as the 'flour makes her over'. Now, the mother's 'hairs' and wrinkles on her cheek' are covered with flour making her countenance more glamorous. Though the poet feels pain at the sight of the mother, the illusions created in his mind of the mother's beauty engages him in some pleasant feeling to forget the present. Thereof, the poet movingly conveys his heavy thoughts of aging and monotony of mother's life in the poem.

In the second septet of the poem, the poet converges his lenses of observations on his father who fights the harsh weather. The speaker grieves to witness his 'Dad' who 'soaks himself in the rain'. The tough luck of the father 'goes' again to work 'on a hole that reappears every Winter'. The nature unsettles the father making his situation worse and demanding physical strain in his old age. The choice of informal diction 'Dad' suggests that the poet's affableness with his father more than his mother. The description of winter as recurring trouble for the father implies cold treatment of the nature and father's struggle to make the ends meet. The images of 'hedges and blackthorn' provides a country setting of poet's Home. Thus, the speaker conveys his feelings for the struggling old father in cold weather in the countryside.

Further in the description of the father, Sheers conveys the futility of father's efforts and hard work to support the family. The readers note the fact that his father makes living in the routine of countryside. The 'wet wool laced on the edges of the hedges' indicate the livestock the father keeps in the fields. Besides, the image of 'hay' also suggests that the father's hard work in the fields. Despite father's hard work, 'his pockets are filled with filings of hay' but not any good money for his living. Hence, the poet feels painful of his father's situation. 'The filings of hay' stands as symbol of worthlessness despite becoming 'wild' in countenance after hard work. In short, the poet movingly conveys his thoughts of futility in father's life and sorrow for father's predicament and struggle in his old age.

In the end, Sheers dedicates the quatrain to his grandfather. In view of the structure of the poem, only four lines in comparison to septet for parents suggest the few years left in his grandfather's life so the theme of death and mortality emerges in the poem. The poet presents an ironic occasion when 'all seated' for dinner and grandfather 'pours the wine'. To the poet, the joyful get together reminds fast approaching death of his grandfather. The grandfather's 'unsteady hands' signify his growing physical weakness. The poet notices growing inability of the grandfather who cannot make 'the neck of the bottle' reach 'the lip of glass'. Clinking the glass and the bottle in his attempts, grandfather 'shivers' and 'plays' the 'tone faster'; which creates a paradoxical idea as the tune of death. Therefore, the poet movingly expresses and regrets the speedy aging and approaching death of grandfather. In all three cases, the poet adopts euphemistic approach to lighten the mood of the poem and justifies the title of the poem 'Coming Home' a moment to rejoice.

In conclusion, Coming home proves to be painful and unpleasant for the poet who experiences the harsh realities and truth of life. The ideas of mortality and aging hurt him though being young in life but foresees an inevitability.   **Word Count: 919**

14 *STABAT MATER* by Sam Hunt

IGCSE Exam Style Questions:

1. Explore how Hunt vividly portrays the mother's spirit in the poem *Stabat Mater*.

OR

2. Explore how Hunt movingly conveys his feelings for the mother in the poem *Stabat Mater*.

OR

3. In what ways Hunt movingly portrays the mother's feelings in the poem *Stabat Mater*.

OR

4. How does Hunt vividly convey the mother's thoughts and feelings in *Stabat Mater?*

OR

5. In what ways does Hunt create parallelism between his mother and the grieving mother Mary in the poem *Stabat Mater?*

Model Response: A Grade

How does Hunt vividly convey the mother's thoughts and feelings in Stabat Mater?

Hunt , in his sonnet Stabat Mater , unquestionably sings a song in praise of his mother and vividly conveys her thoughts and feelings after being married to a man who senior to her father. Choosing a religious title of sorrowful hymn sung for the mother Mary, the poet draws a parallelism between mother Mary's sorrow at the crucifixion of her son and his young mother's sorrow at her husband's aging. Despite this note of age as a cause of mortification to the mother, the poet observes a greater maturity, exuberance and certain veneration in her towards the relationship beyond the bondage of marriage.

In the first quatrain of the sonnet, Hunt vividly describes the feelings of the mother as observed in her book; a place of her emotional married life is saved in fond memories. He portrays the mother's sorrows in an euphemistic properties yet presenting a realistic situation of a younger girl at the beginning of her marriage to a senior. Unaware of the kind of relationship the mother needs to consider in ' the first few years of married life' with her husband, the poet's 'mother' upholds an extreme formality and etiquette with her husband, 'Mr Hunt'. The title of respect 'Mr' suggests that the mother holds immense regard for him without being put down by the fact that he is a senior for the relationship. However, the irregular rhyme (abcb, defg, hiji, kk), does not continue this spirit rather turns to discomfiture in mood. Thus, the readers note the mother's veneration and regard for her senior husband's age and the stature in their relationship through initial years of marriage.

In the second quatrain, the poet brings forth his mother's mortification and sorrows being felt in the relationship with her senior husband when the poet 'asked why' she 'had inscribed' in her 'book'...'To dear Mr Hunt'. The question of the son makes her feel 'embarrassed' as she needs to explain her situation of being 'small' in front of such an 'elder; to 'her father'. The readers empathise with the mother for the fact that she faces certainly 'hard' circumstances whenever her husband 'made her seem so small' in age for the relationship. However, the spirit and muliebrity of the mother seems to progress with years spent with her senior husband so she becomes a 'loving wife' for the poet's father. The poet conveys the mother's feelings of littleness in age and relationship yet he notes her exuberance and blitheness in the relationship of marriage.

In the third quatrain, the poet turns the poem on a melancholic note. The mother grieves the situation with her 'old' husband. The theme of 'old age' and the need for 'guiding' her husband turns the poem gloomy in mood. Though the readers observe that the path towards death is not far for him as 'he roams old age' in the mother's hands and care, she does not show her sorrows but behaves 'in a different way' and puts up a brave heart as mother Mary experiences during crucifixion of her son Jesus. Though both relationships are different, the poet sees the same agony and sorrow felt in both mothers. The husband lives his second childhood in the hands of the poet's mother who feels same sorrow of mother Mary for her son Jesus at the crucifixion. This note of parallelism emerges from the significance of the title of the poem. In this context, the poet's mother shows positive spirit of 'a girl' but not an aging mother. Thereof, the poet conveys mother's spirit in calling his 'father every other sort of name' for the fact not understanding magnitude of the relationship and its intensity of taking care and 'guiding' him' in his old age rather being in bondage of marriage. The new shift in thought from a lighter mood in first quatrain to seriousness in third quatrain gathers more layers of meaning to understand mother's feelings and thoughts about the relationship.

As with English sonnet's tradition, the couplet of the song creates an epiphanic effect in the marriage relationship of poet's mother. The mother feels that it is God's play and she needs to accept it 'as if it' is a divine relationship made in heaven. 'Sometimes, she turns to' the poet, and advices her son to 'stand up straight' once there comes an acceptance from heart; call it responsibility or relationship. The mother thinks on a philosophical note that 'there's no return' once you are in the 'game' of God and there is only a way to 'learn' but no avoidance as she learns to live with her senior husband despite her being so young and in certain discomfort at heart. In fact, this acceptance of relationship becomes more emotional and bond of love in a few years of marriage; which is the truth of wonder in the poem. Therefore, the readers note that the mother considers her relationship is divine and made in heaven.

In conclusion, the poet evidently establishes certain spiritual meaning in the relationship between his mother and his father. The poet perceives that the grief between two mothers is same though the relationships are different. The mother attains certain greatness in her attitude watching his senior husband who marches towards death as aging gets on him as with mother Mary who attains divinity with Jesus at crucifixion; the time of physically leaving this world. This act of maturation in a young mother draws certain praise and admiration in poet's heart watching and guiding his father.

Word Count: 918

ABOUT THE AUTHOR

Atchula Subrahmanyam is Head of the Department of English at GIIS-Singapore. He is a trained IBDP and IGCSE teacher with 9 years of teaching practice. He is a Postgraduate in English Literature and a trained graduate teacher in English from English and Foreign Languages University, Hyderabad. He also holds Level 4 Certificate in TESOL from Trinity College London; studied at St Giles International Central London. He is also a CIE accredited assessor for ESL Oral Assessment.

CPSIA information can be obtained
at www.ICGtesting.com
Printed in the USA
LVHW031229131218
600169LV00015B/456/P